Bette

C000137075

Meetings

How to Facilitate Virtual Team Meetings in Easy Steps

(A super-short book about what to do before, during, and after your remote meetings so that they're more effective)

by

Hassan Osman

Better Online Meetings: How to Facilitate Virtual Team Meetings in Easy Steps (A super-short book about what to do before, during, and after your remote meetings so that they're more effective)
Copyright © 2020 by Hassan Osman.

Liability Disclaimer and FTC Notice
The purpose of this book is to provide the user with general information about the subject matter presented. This book is for entertainment purposes only. This book is not intended, nor should the user consider it, to be legal advice for a specific situation. The author, company, and publisher make no representations or warranties with respect to the accuracy, fitness, completeness, or applicability of the contents of this book. They disclaim any

Contents

Introduction 5

Your Free Bonus.....................................10

Section I: Before Your Meeting 11

Section II: During Your Meeting..............22

Section III: After Your Meeting 30

Conclusion 35

Thank You!...37

Other Books 38

Introduction

I almost didn't write this book.

Why?

Because most advice about how to run effective meetings is already out there in multiple books, blog posts, and business articles.

Who wants to read yet another resource about the importance of having an agenda or taking meeting minutes?

However, the sheer number of people who were forced to work from home by the coronavirus pandemic resulted in a major surge in online meetings.

And that amplified two main problems we've always had with meetings.

First, we attend way too many meetings (a quantity problem), and second, we attend too many *bad* meetings (a quality problem).

Given that meetings aren't going away anytime soon, I decided to publish this book as a super-short guide to help solve both the quantity problem and the quality one.

If you're fairly new to running online meetings, you'll get lots of value from this book. You'll learn the fundamentals about how to facilitate meetings effectively so that you're successful at leading your remote team.

However, if you're quite experienced at online meetings, then you'll likely know most of what's in this book because the content focuses on common-sense advice. Still, I would encourage you to skim through it—you might pick up a couple of insights that you haven't considered before.

Who is this book for?

This book is for team leaders and managers who run remote meetings in medium- to large-sized organizations. It's also for business owners and entrepreneurs who lead distributed teams.

The content of the book is technology-agnostic, meaning that it doesn't matter if you use Zoom, Webex, GoToMeeting or any other meeting tool. The advice applies regardless of the application you use.

Why should you listen to what I have to say?

I manage projects and project management teams for a living.

I'm currently a Project Management Office (PMO) director at Cisco Systems, where I lead teams on delivering complex technology programs across the US, Canada, and Latin America. (Lawyer-required note: the opinions in this book are mine and not those of Cisco.)

Prior to Cisco, I was a management consultant at Ernst & Young (now EY), where I ran projects and programs at Fortune 100 companies.

I've spent the majority of my career in meetings, and I've experienced firsthand what works and what doesn't during online discussions.

This book contains the best of the best practical advice that will help you run a successful online meeting yourself.

You'll get simple tactics that you can implement straight away to help you prepare, as well as scripts that you can copy and paste to save you time.

How is this book organized?

This book is organized into three main sections. Section I is about what you need to do *before* your meeting, Section II covers what you need to do *during* your meeting, and Section III is about what you need to do *after* your meeting.

Before you start, here are a few things you should know.

First, although some of these steps might seem elementary or redundant, don't skip over any of them. They have been carefully thought out as part of a comprehensive step-by-step process.

Second, the book is intentionally super-short because it's boiled down to its essentials. I didn't want to waste your time with useless padding, so I removed any fluff that didn't add much value.

Third, if you've read any of my previous blog posts or books, then you'll find a lot of the material here similar. That's because I believe in the same few concepts about running meetings effectively.

Finally, I realize that meetings is a boring subject, but meetings are the second-worst time-wasters in your work life (the first is email), so do take this topic seriously. If you follow these steps to the letter, you'll never need to read anything else about meetings again. I guarantee it.

Let's get started.

Your Free Bonus

As a thank you for your purchase, I'm offering a free bonus that is exclusive to my readers.

This bonus includes a couple of templates to help you with your online meeting: a **meeting agenda template** and a **meeting minutes template** that you can use with your team.

The templates match the guidelines in this book, so you will save time in creating your own documents. I'll also explain how to use these templates throughout the book.

The files are in Microsoft Word (.docx) format so that you can start using them right away.

Visit the following page to download your free bonus:

www.thecouchmanager.com/bom-bonus

Section I: Before Your Meeting

In this section, we'll cover the four steps that you need to take before your online meeting. These include: deciding on a need and an objective, determining your attendees, drafting an agenda, defining the remote logistics, and sending your invite along with any reminders.

Step One: Decide on a Need and an Objective

Someone once said, "Just like wars, meetings should be a last resort."

So the first question you should ask yourself before setting up any meeting is: "Do I really need to have this meeting?"

Think really, really hard about that question, and about whether you can write an email, make a quick call, or use some other method instead of having a meeting with your team.

Chances are you can leverage an alternative instead.

Meeting overload is such a common problem that "I survived another meeting that should have been an email" is a popular meme now.

After confirming that you do indeed need a meeting, your next step is to define your objective.

And the objective should be determined *before* you set up the meeting, not during. If you're having difficulty defining a goal, then you probably don't need a meeting.

A simple way to define your objective is to complete the following sentence: "The objective of this meeting is to _____ "

And fill in the blank with a phrase that starts with an action verb:

"decide on…"
"generate ideas about…"
"get status on…"
"make plans for…"

For example, "The objective of this meeting is to decide on a few options regarding our marketing plan."

Step Two: Determine the Attendees and Draft an Agenda

The next step is to think about whom to invite to your meeting.

Individuals are often invited just to "keep them in the loop"; other than that, there is no functional reason for them being there.

I've been in meetings where more than twenty people were invited, but the conversation was applicable to only three of them.

As Jason Fried, co-founder and CEO of Basecamp, once wrote: "If you're going to schedule a meeting that lasts one hour and invite 10 people to attend then it's a ten-hour meeting, not a one-hour meeting."

Inviting a lot of people to a meeting is not only a waste of time for everyone; it also decreases the level of effectiveness among the group.

The general heuristic is that you want to limit the number of attendees so that you can have a very focused and productive meeting. So think about the role that each team member would play before inviting them.

Moreover, every meeting should have an agenda that explains exactly what the meeting is about.

Although "Have an agenda" is probably the most-shared piece of advice about meetings, not many meeting hosts create one.

I think one reason is that people assume that an agenda should be a fancy or formal document, but it doesn't have to be.

An agenda can be as simple as a couple of bullet points or a short paragraph.

When you're writing the agenda, start out with the objective (which you defined in Step 1), and then list out the discussion points you want to focus on.

Begin your list with the top priorities first (the important stuff that absolutely must be covered in your meeting) and then move on to the least important topics.

You can also highlight who will talk about each topic and set time limits for each one. I usually don't worry about that unless I'm dealing with a huge team and need to keep a tight level of control at my meeting. So if you're leading a smaller team, you can skip the name assignments and time limits.

Here's an example of a short agenda:

Purpose: The objective of this meeting is to review the different options of our implementation plan.

Topics:

- *Summary of last week's status (Ana – 5 mins)*
- *Options review of the implementation plan (Scot– 20 mins)*
- *Review of actions & next steps (Bernard – 5 mins)*

Note: At the beginning of the book, I mentioned that I've included a free meeting agenda template (which includes a bit more detail) that you can download and use with your own team; here's the link again if you haven't downloaded it.

www.thecouchmanager.com/bom-bonus

Step Three: Define the Remote Logistics

Remote logistics include things like the technology that you're going to use and what time slots you'll consider.

Start out by ensuring that everyone has access to your virtual collaboration tool, such as Webex, Zoom, GoToMeeting, etc. This is especially important for external meetings because people outside your organization might not have the right security permissions to use your preferred tool.

Then decide on whether you want to use video for your online meeting so that attendees can prepare ahead of time. My preference is to always use video conferencing for remote teams because it increases the levels of intimacy and cohesion. However, you should provide an audio-only dial-in option for team members who can't (or don't want to) use video.

Then pick a time-zone-friendly date and time for your team. With remote teams, particularly global teams, it's sometimes a challenge to find a time that works for everyone.

There are several free tools that help you organize your meeting time. For example, *Time and Date AS* (*www.timeanddate.com*) plugs in the date as well as the time zones of your different team members, then provides you with business-friendly times. The best part about this free tool is that it factors in global daylight saving times for you.

Here are a few scheduling guidelines to help you set up your meeting.

- **Tip One: Shorten the Meeting Time**: Most one-hour meetings can be completed in 45 or even 30 minutes. So if you don't absolutely *need* the full hour, then think about starting with the minimum amount of time needed.
- **Tip Two: Have Fewer Meetings**: Similarly, when you need to set up multiple meetings about a particular topic, start with the *minimum* number of meetings to get the job done. For recurring meetings (such as status or standing meetings), schedule fewer meetings and add more if you need to – don't do it the other way around.
- **Tip Three: Batch on the Same Day**: Try to batch your meetings (especially recurring meetings) on the same day of the week. This minimizes the

number of interruptions, the loss of productivity, and the cost associated with switching between work time and meeting time. Your team members will thank you because they will have a higher chance of being more productive during the rest of the week. Tuesday is usually the best day for meetings because it is early in the work week but not too early (like Monday).

- **Tip Four: Batch during the Same Part of the Day**: Try to batch meetings during the same part of the day as well. Choose either mornings or afternoons, but avoid doing both because having one meeting in the morning and another meeting in the afternoon of a single day will disrupt the entire day. The general heuristic is to batch meetings in the early mornings because this will give team members the rest of the day to focus on their tasks.
- **Tip Five: Think about Spacing**: Put some thought into the spacing between meetings and how much time is available for folks to work on tasks before their next meeting. For example, it doesn't make sense to have a status meeting on Friday afternoon and another one on a Monday morning if no one is working

over the weekend. Also, avoid back-to-back meetings for productivity purposes: at a minimum, have at least 30 minutes between meetings to consolidate notes and send emails, and to give yourself a mental break.

Finally, make sure you appoint a leader for your meeting.

Every meeting should have a designated leader who is responsible for moderating the meeting, achieving the stated objectives, and capturing any notes.

Usually, that leader would be you (as the facilitator of the online meeting), but, in some cases, you might assign that role or a separate note-taking role to someone else.

Step Four: Send the Invite, Agenda, and Reminders

The last step is to send out the meeting invite along with the agenda.

As you set up your meeting in the collaboration tool, make sure you use a descriptive title that makes clear to your recipients what the topic is about.

Following this best practice means that people can see at a glance what the meeting is about when they view it in their calendar. For example, instead of using a generic label such as "Discussion," be more specific by stating: "Discussion re July 16 conference logistics."

And if there are any materials or documents that attendees need to review before the meeting, send all that information along with the invite so that everyone comes prepared.

You should also mention the technology requirements (e.g., tool access) and any video vs. audio requirements.

For example, "Team—If you haven't used [Webex/Zoom/other collaboration tool] before, please join a few minutes early to download the plugin because it might take a little bit of time to load for you. Also, please note that we'll be using video during the meeting, so kindly be prepared to turn on your camera. Thank you."

As you get closer to the meeting date, you might want to send out courtesy reminders so that your attendees can go over any material you want them to review prior to the meeting.

For example, "Team—So that we have an effective meeting and don't waste everyone's time, please make sure that you read the financial report and come up with potential solutions before you show up on Friday. Thanks."

Note: Some business leaders, such as Amazon CEO Jeff Bezos, don't trust that people will show up to a meeting prepared, even after they send them multiple reminders and explain why it's important. So, instead of asking people to do any work before the meeting, they factor in 10 to 15 minutes of reading time at the beginning of the meeting to force people to review the material in silence before discussing it. This is a smart way to ensure that everyone is on the same page and that no one can use the "I was too busy to read" alibi. If you decide to try this out yourself, just remember to factor that time into your agenda.

After sending the invite, agenda, and any reminders, the next step is to conduct your meeting.

Section II: During Your Meeting

In this section, we'll cover the steps that you need to take *during* your online meeting. These include welcoming the attendees, covering the ground rules, running through the agenda, capturing meeting minutes, and closing with a review.

Step One: Join Early and Cover the Ground Rules

When you start the meeting, try to join a few minutes early. This allows you to check that the technology is working correctly and gives you some time to make any changes.

Note: If you've never used your collaboration tool (e.g., Webex, Zoom, etc.) prior to setting up the call, then test it with a colleague a few days before your meeting to make sure it works and that you're comfortable with all its important features. This sounds obvious, but I've been in meetings where meeting hosts wasted 15+ minutes because they were trying to learn how everything worked as a new user.

Joining early also ensures that you're on time when the meeting starts and shows everyone that you're leading by example.

If someone else joins early, you can use that opportunity to check with them that your audio, video, and presentation slides are coming across clearly.

Then start welcoming individuals as they join. And when you have a quorum, do a quick roll call of the attendees.

A roll call is especially helpful when you have users who dial in remotely via audio-only (these usually show up as "call-in users" on your collaboration tool) as otherwise neither you nor they can tell who's joined the meeting. It's also best practice to mention everyone's name on the call when multiple people dial in to the same number from a joint conference room.

For example: "Thank you all for joining. We have Mike, Sam, and Jessica on the call, as well as David, who is showing up on the participant list as "Call-in User 1," and Sara, who is showing up as "Call-in User 2." We also have Dani, Adam, and Kelly dialing in together from our conference room in the Boston office."

You should also cover any quick ground rules or housekeeping items, such as asking everyone to "go on mute" to avoid background noises, or to postpone their questions until the end so that you have enough time to cover the material.

Finally, if you're going to record your meeting, it's a good idea to ask for everyone's permission before you start recording. Some people might want to make a few off-the-record comments. And if everyone agrees, state something like "I'm recording the meeting now" after you hit the record button. This ensures that everyone heard you and that you're compliant with any local laws or policies (in some countries or states, it might be illegal to record a meeting if you're not clear with your participants about doing this).

Step Two: Run Through the Agenda

When you formally begin the meeting, start by talking about the objective and state the outcome you want to achieve from that meeting.

Simply restate your objective statement from Step 1 ("The objective of this meeting is to...") and walk through the rest of the agenda. Then explain to your team members what you expect them to talk about or discuss.

If anyone joins late, avoid repeating information unless it's absolutely necessary. It's best to carry on with your meeting to avoid wasting time. The straggler can be brought up to speed later through the meeting minutes.

As you facilitate the meeting, stick to the agenda items and hold people accountable to their time limits. Don't allow anyone to stray off in a different direction.

You can use the agenda as grounds for making sure that everyone remains on topic and asking individuals to take any side conversations offline. This sounds like an obvious step, but few meeting facilitators do it (probably because they don't want to offend anyone).

One thing to point out here is that part of your responsibility as the facilitator is to be inclusive of everyone's opinion where it matters. If you feel that someone's voice is being overshadowed by other, more vocal team members, make sure you give them a fair chance at sharing their thoughts and ideas. A simple statement such as "Hey Janet, we haven't heard what you think about this. What's your point of view?"

helps encourage them to speak up.

Step Three: Capture the Meeting Minutes

Meeting minutes are the notes that summarize your meeting. They include things such as decisions that were made as well as descriptions of your next steps.

You should capture meeting minutes so that your attendees can have a quick reference to go back to. These minutes also summarize the main points for invitees who could not attend.

Here are a few things you should consider capturing as part of your minutes:

1) Meeting details: The general details of your meeting, such as the date, time, attendee list, and host name.

2) Ideas and decisions: Any high-level ideas that were discussed, as well as any decisions that were made during the meeting (preferably along with the name of the decision-maker(s) listed next to each decision).

3) Issues: Any problems or challenges that you are currently encountering.

4) Risks: Any problems or challenges that you might encounter in the future.

5) Action items: The tasks that the team needs to work on next (which could be related to a decision, risk, or issue).

6) Future topics: Any topics that you want to include in future meetings.

7) Supporting information: Any information that supports your minutes, such as a meeting recording link or other references for your attendees.

You don't have to include every single one of those items listed above in your meeting minutes. Use what makes sense to you and your team. However, if you list out any action items, then make sure you assign owners *and* deadlines to each one of them so that you can hold your team members accountable for getting things done.

Some facilitators use meeting recordings (video and/or audio) instead of meeting minutes. I personally don't like that idea. My view is that a meeting recording does not qualify as a substitute for meeting minutes because people don't have the time to re-watch an entire meeting. And even if they do, they might not be 100% clear on what actions they need to take. So it's a better idea to capture meeting minutes.

Similarly, there are Artificial Intelligence (AI) tools that help transcribe meetings for you. While those might help save you some time, a transcription alone doesn't qualify as meeting minutes for the same reasons as meeting recordings (people have no time to read and they need some guidance on actions and decisions).

Note: The free bonus I referred to at the beginning of the book also includes a sample meeting minutes template (in MS Word format) that you can copy and paste and use with your team.

Visit the following link it if you didn't already:

www.thecouchmanager.com/bom-bonus

Step Four: Close with a Review

A best practice is to set aside five minutes at the end of your meeting to do a full review of the notes you took.

If you run out of time during your meeting (to cover what you wanted to cover in the agenda), it's still a better idea to end a couple of minutes early to do a review instead of carrying on with other agenda items.

As the meeting ends, do a full review of the notes you took.

Start with the action items first, and verbally confirm the tasks, their assigned owners, and their deadlines.

Then, if you have some time remaining, go over the decisions, risks, and issues that were discussed.

Summarizing what was said in the meeting before it ends is the best way to increase the chances that things will get done and that there is no confusion about the meeting's output.

Section III: After Your Meeting

In this final section, we'll cover the two steps that you need to take *after* you complete your online meeting. These include distributing the meeting minutes and following up on your action items.

Step One: Distribute the Meeting Minutes

After the meeting is over, distribute the meeting minutes to your attendees. Make sure you also include any invitees who couldn't attend the meeting, as well as any other relevant stakeholders who might be interested in being informed. For example, you might want to copy your own boss (even if they were not expected to attend) to keep them in the loop on the latest status.

You could also upload the meeting minutes to a document repository for future reference.

While there's some debate about whether meeting minutes are effective (most people don't really read them), they might be necessary (or even required) in some projects to track issues if they surface later on.

After the meeting is over, you should also follow up with a written summary that highlights explicitly who is working on what and when everything is due.

Although those action items would already be listed in the meeting minutes document that you distributed, there are many benefits in highlighting them separately in an email.

One best practice is to send out an email with an action list and include the meeting minutes as an attachment (in MS Word or PDF format) to minimize the number of emails you send out.

Here's what your email should include:

- **A quick summary**: Start your message with a high-level summary of the meeting.
- **Meeting minutes**: Include a copy of your meeting minutes, which should consist of your detailed notes as well as a description of the actions, issues, and risks that came up during the meeting. If you recorded the session, then include a link to the recording in your meeting minutes as well.

- **Summary of immediate next steps**: Again, although the meeting minutes should already include the next steps that everyone should take, it's a good idea to summarize the immediate next steps in the body of your email so that no one misses them.
- **Relevant links or attachments**: Include any links that you referenced in the meeting, as well as any attachments (such as PowerPoint slides) that you discussed.

Here's a sample script of an update:

Team,

Thank you all for attending the meeting on <Date> at <Time>. The purpose of the meeting was to <meeting objective>.

Attached is the PowerPoint deck that we reviewed during the call.

I have also attached a meeting minutes file, which includes a summary of what was discussed during the meeting, as well as the next steps of our project. The meeting minutes also include a link to the recording of the meeting.

Here's a quick summary of our immediate next steps:

- *<Action>, <Action Owner>, <Due Date>*
- *<Action>, <Action Owner>, <Due Date>*
- *<Action>, <Action Owner>, <Due Date>*

And here are the links to our document repository as well as the collaboration tool. Please make sure you sign up to an account on both platforms as soon as possible so that we start using them as a team.

- *<Collaboration tool link>*
- *<Document repository link>*

Thanks again for your time. If you have any questions, please feel free to reach out to me directly.

Thank you,

Hassan Osman

Step Two: Follow Up on Action Items

Your last task is to follow up on all the next steps that you highlighted in your email and meeting minutes.

Unless you have a time-sensitive reason for

following up immediately, it's best to wait a few days before asking anyone for updates so that the team has enough time to work on their tasks.

If you had any action items assigned to you, then it's also a good idea to list your own update as you ask for updates from the team.

Example: "All—I'd like to follow up on the actions listed below. Can each of you please send me a quick status on where you are with those? Regarding Task X that was assigned to me, I'm nearly done with it and should be able to send the report out in a couple of days."

A best practice is to keep track of the status of all action items, risks, and issues that are assigned to your team by capturing them in writing. This could be in another document repository tool or a spreadsheet. Where the information is posted doesn't matter as much as making sure it's listed *somewhere* for reference.

Finally, if your next meeting is related to the same topic (such as a recurring staff or status meeting), then it's a good idea to start your next meeting with the latest status of the open items from your last meeting.

Conclusion

We just covered how to run a successful online meeting in easy steps, and what you need to do before, during, and after your meeting.

To summarize, here's what you should do before every meeting:

1. Decide on a need and an objective.
2. Determine the attendees and draft an agenda.
3. Define the remote logistics
4. Send the invite, agenda and reminders.

Here's what you should do during each meeting:

1. Join early and cover the ground rules.
2. Run through the agenda.
3. Capture the meeting minutes.
4. Close with a review.

And, finally, here's what you should do after each meeting:

1. Distribute the meeting minutes.
2. Follow up on action items.

If you follow those steps with each team

meeting, I'll guarantee that you will end up having not only better meetings but, most importantly, fewer meetings.

Thank You!

I want to thank you once again for purchasing this book. I hope you found it helpful, and I wish you the best of luck with your team meetings.

I'd like to ask you for a small favor.

If you enjoyed the book, I'd be very grateful if you would leave an honest review on Amazon (I read them all).

Every single review counts, and your support really does make a difference.

Thanks again for your kind support!

Cheers,

Hassan

Other Books

I write short books for busy managers. If you enjoyed this book, you'd probably enjoy one of my other publications below.

You can find any of those books by searching for the book title on Amazon.com

Don't Reply All

An Amazon #1 Best Selling book about 18 tactics that will help you write better emails and improve communication with your team.

"Hassan has masterfully compiled a set of real-world tips & tricks that can be actioned against immediately. This book is packed with practical advice for everyone."

*- **Larry Gioia**, Director, Health Industries Advisory at PwC*

Fun Virtual Team-Building Activities

A short book that includes 18 easy games and activities that help your remote team stay connected while they work from home (no special software needed; includes downloadable templates).

"Staying connected while working remotely isn't easy, but in this short book, Hassan Osman harnesses his years of experience to compile some practical and non-obvious suggestions for getting closer to your colleagues using the tools you already have. Your team can bond virtually, and this helpful guide will help you do it."

- **Rohit Bhargava**, *Founder of the Non-Obvious Guide Series*

Influencing Virtual Teams

An Amazon #1 Best Seller that will help you manage your team more effectively. It's a quick read and includes 17 tactics that help you get things done with your remote employees.

"The book includes many immediately actionable ideas for managing a distributed team. Clarity and efficiency of communication is paramount in a virtual environment and Hassan has honed in on the key tactics that will make a big difference in your work day."

- **Tom Moor**, *Co-founder of Buffer*

Effective Delegation of Authority

A (really) short book for new managers about how to delegate work using a simple delegation process. You'll learn how to manage your employees in simple steps.

"So many managers fail at delegation, a core essential for handling complexity in every organization. In this concise and practical guide, Hassan Osman shows us the steps he's used to get results as an experienced leader. This quick read is a must for new managers -- and also for senior managers who are seeking a framework to help newer managers avoid the common mistakes."

- **Dave Stachowiak**, *Host of the "Coaching for Leaders" Podcast*

Printed in Great Britain
by Amazon